milk and
honey

rupi kaur

Andrews McMeel
Publishing®

copyright

Andrews McMeel Publishing

a division of Andrews McMeel Universal

1130 Walnut Street, Kansas City, Missouri 64106

www.andrewsmcmeel.com

www.rupikaur.com

ISBN: 978-1-4494-7866-7

Library of Congress Control Number: 2015946719

Ebook by Erika Kuster

ATTENTION: SCHOOLS AND BUSINESSES

Andrews McMeel books are available at quantity discounts with bulk purchase for educational, business, or sales promotional use. For information, please e-mail the Andrews McMeel Publishing Special Sales Department: special-sales@amuniversal.com.

**for
the arms
that hold me**

my heart woke me crying last night
how can i help i begged
my heart said
write the book

contents

the
hurting

how is it so easy for you
to be kind to people *he asked*

milk and honey dripped
from my lips as i answered

cause people have not
been kind to me

the first boy that kissed me
held my shoulders down
like the handlebars of
the first bicycle
he ever rode
i was five

he had the smell of
starvation on his lips
which he picked up from
his father feasting on his mother at 4 a.m.

he was the first boy
to teach me my body was
for giving to those that wanted
that i should feel anything
less than whole

and my god
did i feel as empty
as his mother at 4:25 a.m.

you
have been
taught youe legs
are a pit stop for men
that need a place to rest
a vacant body empty enough
for gueste but no one
ever comes and is
wiling to
stay

it is your blood
in my veins
tell me how i'm
supposed to forget

the therapist places
the doll in front of you
it is the size of girls
your uncles like touching

point to where his hands were

you point to the spot
between its legs the one
he fingered out of you
like a confession

how're you feeling

you pull the lump
in your throat out
with your teeth
and say *fine*
numb really

- midweek sessions

he was supposed to be
the first male love of your life
you still search for him
everywhere

- *father*

you were so afraid
 of my voice
 i decided to be
 afraid of it too

she was a rose
in the hands of those
who had no intention
of keeping her

every time you
tell your daughter
you yell at her
out of love
you teach her to confuse
anger with kindness
which seems like a good idea
till she grows up to
trust men who hurt her
cause they look so much
like you

- to fathers with daughters

i've had sex she said
but i don't know
what making love
feels like

if i knew what
safety looked like
i would have spent
less time falling into
arms that were not

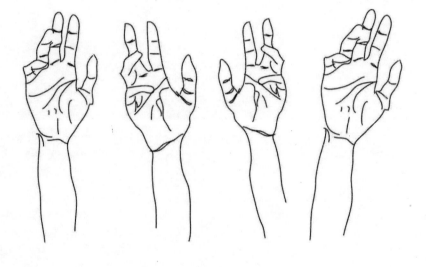

sex takes the consent of two
if one person is lying there not doing anything
cause they are not ready
or not in the mood
or simply don't want to
yet the other is having sex
with their body it's not love
it is rape

the idea that we are
so capable of love
but still choose
to be toxic

there is no bigger illusion in the world
than the idea that a woman will
bring dishonor into a home
if she tries to keep her heart
and her body safe

you pinned
my legs to
the ground
with your feet
and demanded
i stand up

the rape will
tear you
in half

but it
will not
end you

you have sadness
 living in places
  sadness shouldn't live

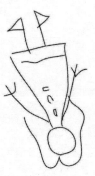

a daughter should
not have to
beg her father
for a relationship

trying to convince myself
 i am allowed
 to take up space
 is like writing with
 my left hand
 when i was born
 to use my right

- the idea of shrinking is hereditary

you tell me to quiet down cause
my opinions make me less beautiful
but i was not made with a fire in my belly
so i could be put out
i was not made with a lightness on my tongue
so i could be easy to swallow
i was made heavy
half blade and half silk
difficult to forget and not easy
for the mind to follow

he guts her
with his fingers
like he's scraping
the inside of a
cantaloupe clean

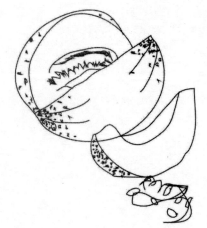

your mother
is in the habit of
offering more love
than you can carry

your father is absent

you are a war
the border between two countries
the collateral damage
the paradox that joins the two
but also splits them apart

emptying out of my mother's belly
was my first act of disappearance
learning to shrink for a family
who likes their daughters invisible
was the second
the art of being empty
is simple
believe them when they say
you are nothing
repeat it to yourself
like a wish
i am nothing
i am nothing
i am nothing
so often
the only reason you know
you're still alive is from the
heaving of your chest

- the art of being empty

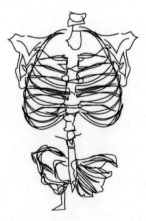

24

you look just like your mother

     i guess i do carry her tenderness well

you both have the same eyes

     cause we are both exhausted

and the hands

     we share the same wilting fingers

but that rage your mother doesn't wear that anger

     you're right
     this rage is the one thing
     i get from my father

(homage to warsan shire's inheritance)

when my mother opens her mouth
to have a conversation at dinner
my father shoves the word hush
between her lips and tells her to
never speak with her mouth full
this is how the women in my family
learned to live with their mouths closed

our knees
pried open
by cousins
and uncles
and men
our bodies touched
by all the wrong people
that even in a bed full of safety
we are afraid

father. you always call to say nothing in particular. you ask what i'm doing or where i am and when the silence stretches like a lifetime between us i scramble to find questions to keep the conversation going. what i long to say most is. i understand this world broke you. it has been so hard on your feet. i don't blame you for not knowing how to remain soft with me. sometimes i stay up thinking of all the places you are hurting which you'll never care to mention. i come from the same aching blood. from the same bone so desperate for attention i collapse in on myself. i am your daughter. i know the small talk is the only way you know how to tell me you love me. cause it is the only way i know how to tell you.

you plough into me with two fingers and i am mostly shocked. it feels like rubber against an open wound. i do not like it. you begin pushing faster and faster. but i feel nothing. you search my face for a reaction so i begin acting like the naked women in the videos you watch when you think no one's looking. i imitate their moans. hollow and hungry. you ask if it feels good and i say yes so quickly it sounds rehearsed. but the acting. you do not notice.

the thing about having
an alcoholic parent
is an alcoholic parent
does not exist

simply
an alcoholic
who could not stay sober
long enough to raise their kids

i can't tell if my mother is
terrified or in love with
my father it all
looks the same

i flinch when you touch me
i fear it is him

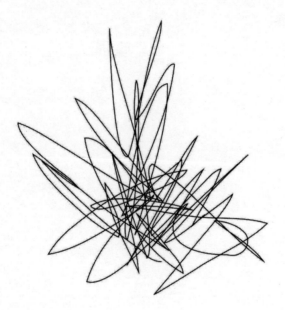

the
loving

when my mother was pregnant
with her second child i was four
i pointed at her swollen belly confused at how
my mother had gotten so big in such little time
my father scooped me in his tree trunk arms and
said the closest thing to god on this earth
is a woman's body it's where life comes from
and to have a grown man tell me something
so powerful at such a young age
changed me to see the entire universe
rested at my mother's feet

i struggle so deeply
to understand
how someone can
pour their entire soul
blood and energy
into someone
without wanting
anything in
return

- i will have to wait till i'm a mother

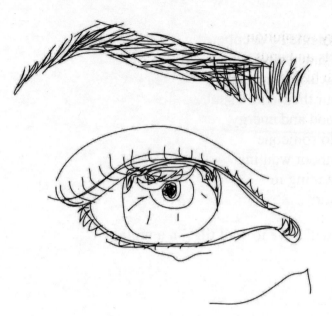

no
it won't
be love at
first sight when
we meet it'll be love
at first remembrance cause
i've seen you in my mother's eyes
when she tells me to marry the type
of man i'd want to raise my son to be like

every revolution
starts and ends
with his lips

what am i to you *he asks*
i put my hands in his lap
and whisper you
are every hope
i've ever had
in human form

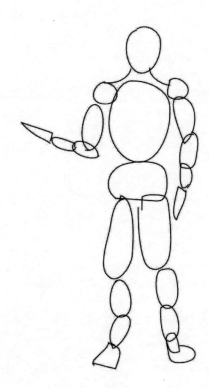

my favorite thing about you is your smell
you smell like
earth
herbs
gardens
a little more
human than the rest of us

i know i
should crumble
for better reasons
but have you seen
that boy he brings
the sun to its
knees every
night

you are the faint line
between faith and
blindly waiting

- *letter to my future lover*

nothing is safer
than the sound of you
reading out loud to me

- *the perfect date*

he placed his hands
on my mind
before reaching
for my waist
my hips
or my lips
he didn't call me
beautiful first
he called me
exquisite

- *how he touches me*

i am learning
how to love him
by loving myself

he says
i am sorry i am not an easy person to want
i look at him surprised
who said i wanted easy
i don't crave easy
i crave goddamn difficult

the very thought of you
has my legs spread apart
like an easel with a canvas
begging for art

i am ready for you
i have always
been
ready for you

- the first time

i do not want to have you
to fill the empty parts of me
i want to be full on my own
i want to be so complete
i could light a whole city
and then
i want to have you
cause the two of us combined
could set it on fire

love will come
and when love comes
love will hold you
love will call your name
and you will melt
sometimes though
love will hurt you but
love will never mean to
love will play no games
cause love knows life
has been hard enough already

i'd be lying if i said
you make me speechless
the truth is you make my
tongue so weak it forgets
what language to speak in

he asks me what i do
i tell him i work for a small company
that makes packaging for—
he stops me midsentence
no not what you do to pay the bills
what drives you crazy
what keeps you up at night

i tell him *i write*
he asks me to show him something
i take the tips of my fingers
place them inside his forearm
and graze them down his wrist
goose bumps rise to the surface
i see his mouth clench
muscles tighten
his eyes pore into mine
as though i'm the reason
for making them blink
i break gaze just as
he inches toward me
i step back

so that's what you do
you command attention
my cheeks flush as
i smile shyly
confessing
i can't help it

51

you might not have been my first love
but you were the love that made
all the other loves
irrelevant

you've touched me
without even
touching me

how do you turn
a forest fire like me
so soft i turn into
running water

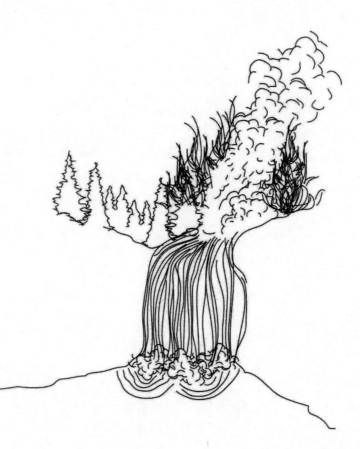

you look like you smell of
honey and no pain
let me have a taste of that

your name is
the strongest
positive and negative
connotation in any language
it either lights me up or
leaves me aching for days

you talk too much
he whispers into my ear
i can think of better ways to use that mouth

it's your voice
  that undresses me

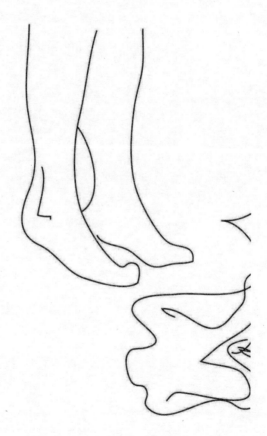

my name sounds so good
french kissing your tongue

you wrap your fingers
 around my hair
 and pull
 this
 is how you make
 music out of me

- foreplay

on days
 like this
i need you to
run your fingers
through my hair
and speak softly

- *you*

i want your hands
to hold
not my hands
your lips
to kiss
not my lips
but other places

i need someone
who knows struggle
as well as i do
someone
willing to hold my feet in their lap
on days it is too difficult to stand
the type of person who gives
exactly what i need
before i even know i need it
the type of lover who hears me
even when i do not speak
is the type of understanding
i demand

- the type of lover i need

you move my hand
 between my legs
 and whisper
make those pretty little fingers dance for me

- solo performance

we've been arguing more than we ought to. about things neither of us remember or care about cause that's how we avoid the bigger questions. instead of asking why we don't say *i love you* to one another as often as we used to. we fight about things like: who was supposed to get up and turn the lights off first. or who was supposed to pop the frozen pizza in the oven after work. taking hits at the most vulnerable parts of one another. we're like fingers on thorns honey. we know exactly where it hurts.

and everything is on the table tonight. like that one time you whispered a name i'm pretty sure wasn't mine in your sleep. or last week when you said you were working late. so i called work but they said you'd already left a couple hours ago. where were you for those couple hours.

i know. i know. your excuses make all the sense in the world. and i get a little carried away for no good reason and eventually begin crying. but what else do you expect baby. i love you so much. i'm sorry i thought you were lying.

that's when you hold your head with your hands in frustration. half begging me to stop. half tired and sick of it. the toxin in our mouths has burnt holes in our cheeks. we look less alive than we used to. less color in our faces. but don't kid yourself. no matter how bad it gets we both know you still wanna nail me to the ground.

especially when i'm screaming so loud our fighting wakes the neighbors. and they come running to the door to save us. baby don't open it.

instead. lie me down. lay me open like a map. and with your finger trace the places you still want to **** out of me. kiss me like i am the center point of gravity and you are falling into me like my soul is the focal point of yours. and when your mouth is kissing not my mouth but other places. my legs will split apart out of habit. and that's when. i pull you in. welcome you. home.

when the entire street is looking out their windows wondering what all the commotion is. and the fire trucks come rolling in to save us but they can't distinguish whether these flames began with our anger or our passion. i will smile. throw my head back. arch my body like a mountain you want to split in half. baby lick me.

like your mouth has the gift of reading and i'm your favorite book. find your favorite page in the soft spot between my legs and read it carefully. fluently. vividly. don't you dare leave a single word untouched. and i swear my ending will be so good. the last few words will come. running to your mouth. and when you're done. take a seat. cause it's my turn to make music with my knees pressed to the ground.

sweet baby. this. is how we pull language out of one another with the flick of our tongues. this is how we have the conversation. this. is how we make up.

- how we make up

the
breaking

i always
get myself
into this mess
i always let him
tell me i am beautiful
and half believe it
i always jump think-
ing
he will catch me
and the fall
i am hopelessly
a lover and
a dreamer and
that will be the
death of me

when my mother says i deserve better
i snap to your defense out of habit
he still loves me i shout
she looks at me with defeated eyes
the way a parent looks at their child
when they know this is the type of pain
even they can't fix
and says
it means nothing to me if he loves you
if he can't do a single wretched thing about it

you were so distant
i forgot you were there at all

you said. if it is meant to be. fate will bring us back togeth-
er. for a second i wonder if you are really that naive. if you
really believe fate works like that. as if it lives in the sky
staring down at us. as if it has five fingers and spends its
time placing us like pieces of chess. as if it is not the choic-
es we make. who taught you that. tell me. who convinced
you. you've been given a heart and a mind that isn't yours
to use. that your actions do not define what will become of
you. i want to scream and shout *it's us you fool. we're the
only ones that can bring us back together.* but instead i sit
quietly. smiling softly through quivering lips thinking. isn't
it such a tragic thing. when you can see it so clearly but the
other person doesn't.

don't mistake
salt for sugar
if he wants to
be with you
he will
it's that simple

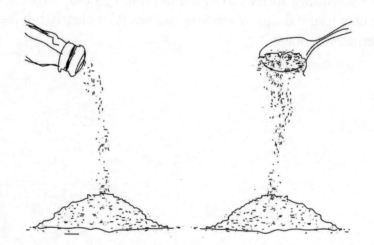

he only whispers *i love you*
as he slips his hands
down the waistband
of your pants

this is where you must
understand the difference
between want and need
you may want that boy
but you certainly
don't need him

you were temptingly beautiful
but stung when i got close

the woman who comes after me will be a bootleg version of who i am. she will try and write poems for you to erase the ones i've left memorized on your lips but her lines could never punch you in the stomach the way mine did. she will then try to make love to your body. but she will never lick, caress, or suck like me. she will be a sad replacement of the woman you let slip. nothing she does will excite you and this will break her. when she is tired of falling apart for a man that doesn't give back what he takes she will recognize me in your eyelids staring at her with pity and it'll hit her. how can she love a man who is busy loving someone he can never get his hands on again.

the next time you
have your coffee black
you'll taste the bitter
state he left you in
it will make you weep
but you'll never
stop drinking
you'd rather have the
darkest parts of him
than have nothing

more than anything
i want to save you
from myself

you have spent enough nights
with his manhood curled inside your legs
to forget what loneliness feels like

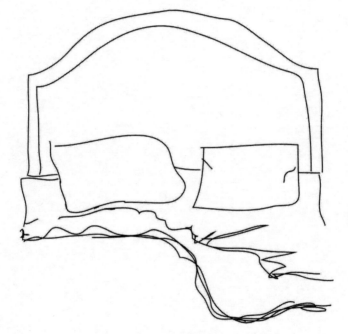

you whisper
i love you
what you mean is
i don't want you to leave

that's the
thing about love
it marinates your lips
till the only word your
mouth remembers
is his name

it must hurt to know
i am your most
beautiful
regret

i didn't leave because
i stopped loving you
i left because the longer
i stayed the less
i loved myself

you mustn't have to
make them want you
they must want you themselves

did you think i was a city
big enough for a weekend getaway
i am the town surrounding it
the one you've never heard of
but always pass through
there are no neon lights here
no skyscrapers or statues
but there is thunder
for i make bridges tremble
i am not street meat i am homemade jam
thick enough to cut the sweetest
thing your lips will touch
i am not police sirens
i am the crackle of a fireplace
i'd burn you and you still
couldn't take your eyes off me
cause i'd look so beautiful doing it
you'd blush
i am not a hotel room i am home
i am not the whiskey you want
i am the water you need
don't come here with expectations
and try to make a vacation out of me

the one who arrives after you
will remind me love is
supposed to be soft

he will taste
like the poetry
i wish i could write

if
he can't help but
degrade other women
when they're not looking
if toxicity is central
to his language
he could hold you
in his lap and be soft
honey
that man could feed you sugar and
douse you in rose water
but that still could not
make him sweet

- if you want to know the type of man he is

i am a museum full of art
but you had your eyes shut

you must have known
you were wrong
when your fingers
were dipped inside me
searching for honey that
would not come for you

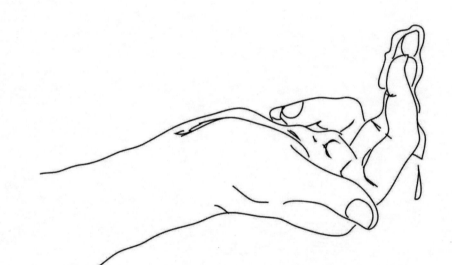

the thing
worth holding on to
would not have let go

when you are broken
and he has left you
do not question
whether you were
enough
the problem was
you were so enough
he was not able to carry it

love made the danger
in you look like safety

even when you undress her
you are searching for me
i am sorry i
taste so good
when the two of you
make love it is
still my name
that rolls off your
tongue accidently

you treat them like they
have a heart like yours
but not everyone can be as
soft and as tender

you don't see the
person they are
you see the person
they have the potential to be

you give and give till
they pull everything out of you
and leave you empty

i had to leave
i was tired of
allowing you to
make me feel
anything less
than whole

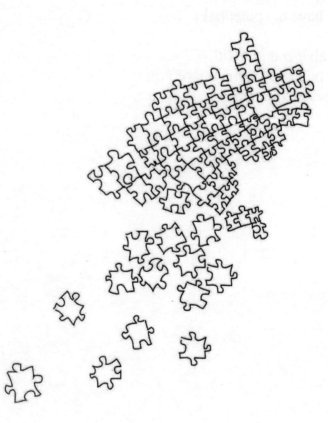

you were the most beautiful thing i'd ever felt till now.
and i was convinced you'd remain the most beautiful thing
i'd ever feel. do you know how limiting that is. to think at
such a ripe young age i'd experienced the most exhilarating
person i'd ever meet. how i'd spend the rest of my life just
settling. to think i'd tasted the rawest form of honey and
everything else would be refined and synthetic. that nothing
beyond this point would add up. that all the years beyond
me could not combine themselves to be sweeter than you.

- falsehood

i don't know what living a balanced life feels like
when i am sad
i don't cry i pour
when i am happy
i don't smile i glow
when i am angry
i don't yell i burn

the good thing about feeling in extremes is
when i love i give them wings
but perhaps that isn't
such a good thing cause
they always tend to leave
and you should see me
when my heart is broken
i don't grieve
i shatter

i came all this way
to give you all these things
but you aren't even looking

the abused
and the
abuser

- *i have been both*

i am undoing you
  from my skin

it wasn't you i was kissing
— don't be mistaken

it was him on my mind
your lips were just convenient

it always comes back to you
boils
circles
itches
its way back to you

i was music
but you had your ears cut off

my tongue is sour
from the hunger of
missing you

i will not have you
build me into your life
when
what i want is to
build a life with you

- *the difference*

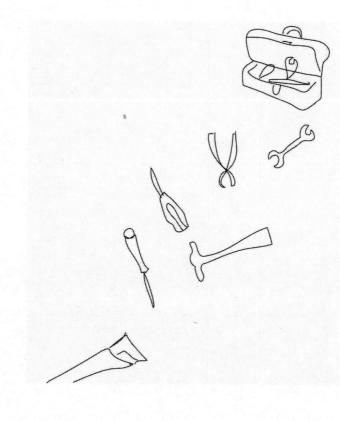

rivers fall from my mouth
tears my eyes can't carry

you are snakeskin
and i keep shedding you somehow
my mind is forgetting
every exquisite detail
of your face
the letting go has
become the forgetting
which is the most
pleasant and saddest thing
to have happened

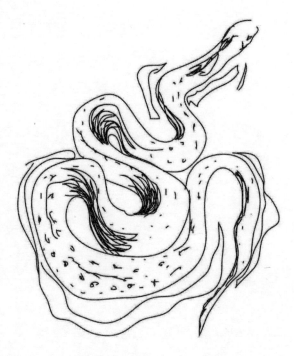

you were not wrong for leaving
you were wrong for coming back
and thinking
you could have me
when it was convenient
and leave when it was not

how can i write
 if he took my hands
 with him

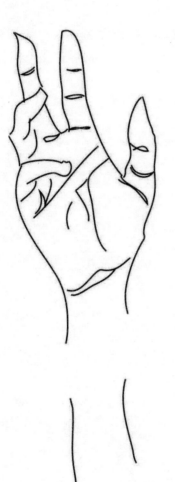
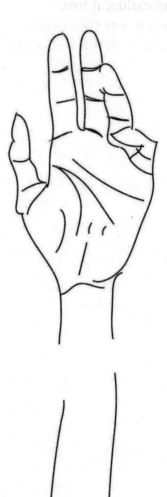

neither of us is happy
but neither of us wants to leave
so we keep breaking one another
and calling it love

we began
with honesty
let us end
in it too

- us

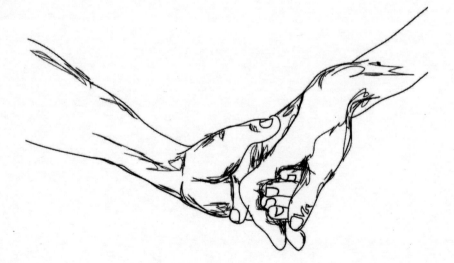

your voice
alone
drives me
to tears

i don't know why
i split myself open
for others knowing
sewing myself up
hurts this much
afterward

people go
but how
they left
always stays

love is not cruel
we are cruel
love is not a game
we have made a game
out of love

how can our love die
if it's written
in these pages

even after the hurt
the loss
the pain
the breaking
your body is still
the only one
i want to be
undressed under

the night after you left
i woke up so broken
the only place to put the pieces
were the bags under my eyes

stay
i whispered
as you
shut the door behind you

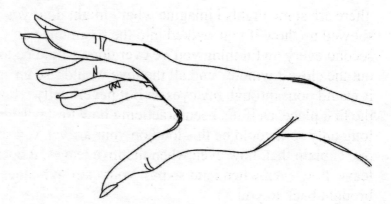

i am confident i am over you. so much that some mornings i wake up with a smile on my face and my hands pressed together thanking the universe for pulling you out of me. thank god i cry. thank god you left. i would not be the empire i am today if you had stayed.

but then.

there are some nights i imagine what i might do if you showed up. how if you walked into the room this very second every awful thing you've ever done would be tossed out the closest window and all the love would rise up again. it would pour through my eyes as if it never really left in the first place. as if it's been practicing how to stay silent so long only so it could be this loud on your arrival. can someone explain that. how even when the love leaves. it doesn't leave. how even when i am so past you. i am so helplessly brought back to you.

he isn't coming back
whispered my head
he has to
sobbed my heart

- wilting

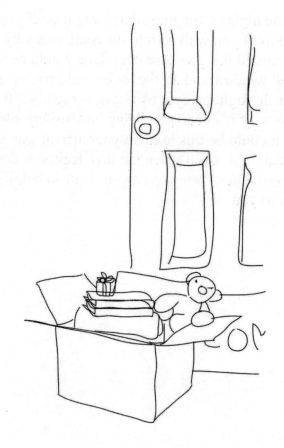

i don't want to be friends
i want all of you

- *more*

i am losing parts of you like i lose eyelashes
unknowingly and everywhere

you cannot leave
and have me too
i cannot exist in
two places at once

- *when you ask if we can still be friends*

i am water

soft enough
to offer life
tough enough
to drown it away

what i miss most is how you loved me. but what i didn't know was how you loved me had so much to do with the person i was. it was a reflection of everything i gave to you. coming back to me. how did i not see that. how. did i sit here soaking in the idea that no one else would love me that way. when it was i that taught you. when it was i that showed you how to fill. the way i needed to be filled. how cruel i was to myself. giving you credit for my warmth simply because you had felt it. thinking it was you who gave me strength. wit. beauty. simply because you recognized it. as if i was already not these things before i met you. as if i did not remain all these once you left.

you leave
but you don't stay gone
why do you do that
why do you
abandon the thing you want to keep
why do you linger
in a place you do not want to stay
why do you think it's okay to do both
go and return all at once

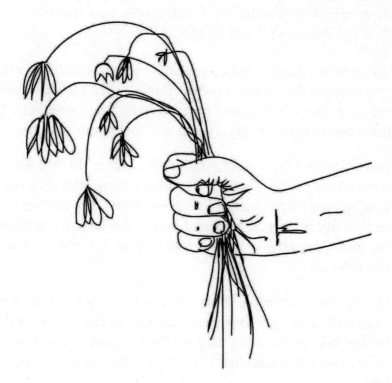

i will tell you about selfish people. even when they know they will hurt you they walk into your life to taste you because you are the type of being they don't want to miss out on. you are too much shine to not be felt. so when they have gotten a good look at everything you have to offer. when they have taken your skin your hair your secrets with them. when they realize how real this is. how much of a storm you are and it hits them.

that is when the cowardice sets in. that is when the person you thought they were is replaced by the sad reality of what they are. that is when they lose every fighting bone in their body and leave after saying *you will find better than me.*

you will stand there naked with half of them still hidden somewhere inside you and sob. asking them why they did it. why they forced you to love them when they had no intention of loving you back and they'll say something along the lines of *i just had to try. i had to give it a chance. it was you after all.*

but that isn't romantic. it isn't sweet. the idea that they were so engulfed by your existence they had to risk breaking it for the sake of knowing they weren't the one missing out. your existence meant that little next to their curiosity of you.

that is the thing about selfish people. they gamble entire beings. entire souls to please their own. one second they are holding you like the world in their lap and the next they have belittled you to a mere picture. a moment. something of the past. one second. they swallow you up and whisper they want to spend the rest of their life with you. but the moment they sense fear. they are already halfway out the door. without having the nerve to let you go with grace. as if the human heart means that little to them.

and after all this. after all of the taking. the nerve. isn't it sad and funny how people have more guts these days to undress you with their fingers than they do to pick up the phone and call. apologize. for the loss. and this is how you lose her.

- *selfish*

to do list (after the breakup):

1. take refuge in your bed.

2. cry. till the tears stop (this will take a few days).

3. don't listen to slow songs.

4. delete their number from your phone even though it is memorized on your fingertips.

5. don't look at old photos.

6. find the closest ice cream shop and treat yourself to two scoops of mint chocolate chip. the mint will calm your heart. you deserve the chocolate.

7. buy new bed sheets.

8. collect all the gifts, t-shirts, and everything with their smell on it and drop it off at a donation center.

9. plan a trip.

10. perfect the art of smiling and nodding when someone brings their name up in conversation.

11. start a new project.

12. whatever you do. do not call.

13. do not beg for what does not want to stay.

14. stop crying at some point.

15. allow yourself to feel foolish for believing you could've built the rest of your life in someone else's stomach.

16. breathe.

the way they
leave
tells you
everything

the
healing

perhaps
i don't deserve
nice things
cause i am paying
for sins i don't
remember

the thing about writing is
i can't tell if it's healing
or destroying me

do not bother holding on to
that thing that does not want you

- *you cannot make it stay*

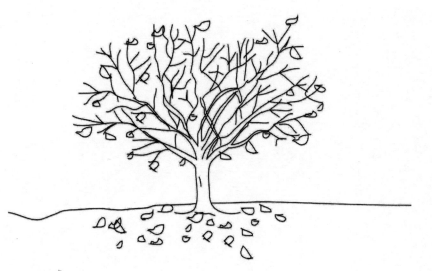

you must enter a relationship
with yourself
before anyone else

accept that you deserve more
than painful love
life is moving
the healthiest thing
for your heart is
to move with it

it is a part of the
human experience to feel pain
do not be afraid
open yourself to it

- *evolving*

loneliness is a sign you are in desperate need of yourself

you are in the habit
of co-depending
on people to
make up for what
you think you lack

who tricked you
into believing
another person
was meant to complete you
when the most they can do is complement

do not look for healing
at the feet of those
who broke you

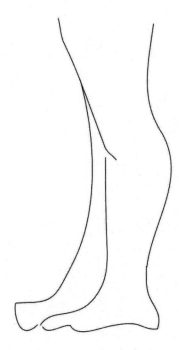

if you were born with
the weakness to fall
you were born with
the strength to rise

perhaps the saddest of all
are those who live waiting
for someone they're not
sure exists

- *7 billion people*

stay strong through your pain
grow flowers from it
you have helped me
grow flowers out of mine so
bloom beautifully
dangerously
loudly
bloom softly
however you need
just bloom

- to the reader

i thank the universe
for taking
everything it has taken
and giving to me
everything it is giving

- *balance*

it takes grace
to remain kind
in cruel situations

fall
in love
with your solitude

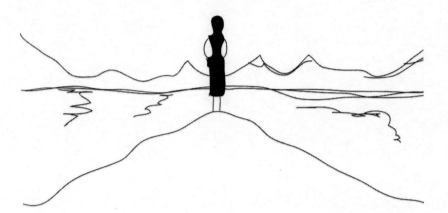

there is a difference between
someone telling you
they love you and
them actually
loving you

sometimes
the apology
never comes
when it is wanted

and when it comes
it is neither wanted
nor needed

- *you are too late*

you tell me
i am not like most girls
and learn to kiss me with your eyes closed
something about the phrase—something about
how i have to be unlike the women
i call sisters in order to be wanted
makes me want to spit your tongue out
like i am supposed to be proud you picked me
as if i should be relieved you think
i am better than them

the next time he
points out the
hair on your legs is
growing back remind
that boy your body
is not his home
he is a guest
warn him to
never outstep
his welcome
again

to be
soft
is
to be
powerful

you deserve to be
completely found
in your surroundings
not lost within them

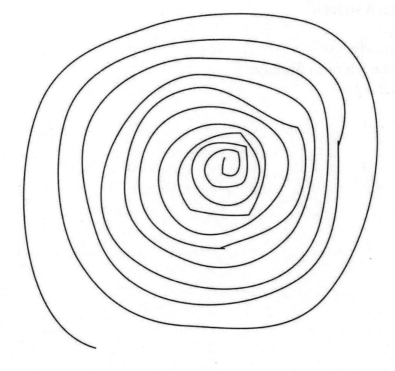

i know it's hard
believe me
i know it feels like
tomorrow will never come
and today will be the most
difficult day to get through
but i swear you will get through
the hurt will pass
as it always does
if you give it time and
let it so let it
go
slowly
like a broken promise
let it go

i like the way the stretch marks
on my thighs look human and
that we're so soft yet
rough and jungle wild
when we need to be
i love that about us
how capable we are of feeling
how unafraid we are of breaking
and tend to our wounds with grace
just being a woman
calling myself
a woman
makes me utterly whole
and complete

my issue with what they consider beautiful
is their concept of beauty
centers around excluding people
i find hair beautiful
when a woman wears it
like a garden on her skin
that is the definition of beauty
big hooked noses
pointing upward to the sky
like they're rising
to the occasion
skin the color of earth
my ancestors planted crops on
to feed a lineage of women with
thighs thick as tree trunks
eyes like almonds
deeply hooded with conviction
the rivers of punjab
flow through my bloodstream so
don't tell me my women
aren't as beautiful
as the ones in
your country

our backs
tell stories
no books have
the spine to
carry

- *women of color*

accept yourself
as you were designed

your body
is a museum
of natural disasters
can you grasp how
stunning that is

losing you
was the becoming
of myself

other women's bodies
  are not our battlegrounds

removing all the hair
off your body is okay
if that's what you want to do
just as much as keeping all the hair
on your body is okay
if that's what you want to do

- *you belong only to yourself*

apparently it is ungraceful of me
to mention my period in public
cause the actual biology
of my body is too real

it is okay to sell what's
between a woman's legs
more than it is okay to
mention its inner workings

the recreational use of
this body is seen as
beautiful while
its nature is
seen as ugly

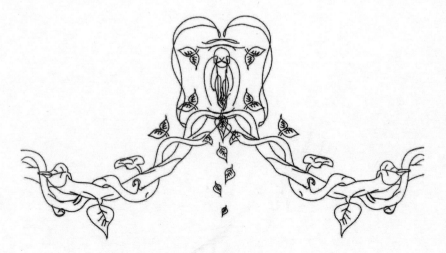

you were a dragon long before
he came around and said
you could fly

you will remain a dragon
long after he's left

i want to apologize to all the women
i have called pretty
before i've called them intelligent or brave
i am sorry i made it sound as though
something as simple as what you're born with
is the most you have to be proud of when your
spirit has crushed mountains
from now on i will say things like
you are resilient or *you are extraordinary*
not because i don't think you're pretty
but because you are so much more than that

i have
 what i have
 and i am happy

 i've lost
 what i've lost
 and i am
 still
 happy

- *outlook*

you look at me and cry
everything hurts

i hold you and whisper
but everything can heal

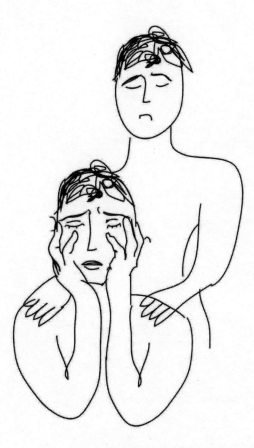

if the hurt comes
so will the happiness

- *be patient*

we are all born
so beautiful

the greatest tragedy is
being convinced we are not

the name kaur
makes me a free woman
it removes the shackles that
try to bind me
uplifts me
to remind me i am equal to
any man even though the state
of this world screams to me i am not
that i am my own woman and
i belong wholly to myself
and the universe
it humbles me
calls out and says i have a
universal duty to share with
humanity to nurture
and serve the sisterhood
to raise those that need raising
the name kaur runs in my blood
it was in me before the word itself existed
it is my identity and my liberation

- kaur
a woman of sikhi

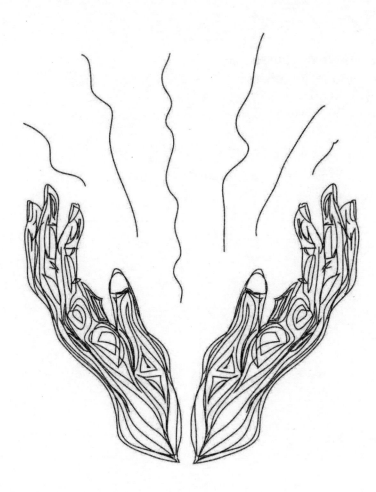

the world
gives you
so much pain
and here you are
making gold out of it

- *there is nothing purer than that*

how you love yourself is
how you teach others
to love you

my heart aches for sisters more than anything
it aches for women helping women
like flowers ache for spring

the goddess between your legs
 makes mouths water

you
 are your own
 soul mate

some people
are so bitter

to them
you must be kindest

we all move forward when
we recognize how resilient
and striking the women
around us are

for you to see beauty here
does not mean
there is beauty in me
it means there is beauty rooted
so deep within you
you can't help but
see it everywhere

hair
if it was not supposed to be there
would not be growing
on our bodies in the first place

- *we are at war with what comes most naturally to us*

most importantly love
like it's the only thing you know how
at the end of the day all this
means nothing
this page
where you're sitting
your degree
your job
the money
nothing even matters
except love and human connection
who you loved
and how deeply you loved them
how you touched the people around you
and how much you gave them

i want to remain so
rooted to the ground
these tears
these hands
these feet
sink in

- *grounded*

you have to stop
searching for why at some point
you have to leave it alone

if you are not enough for yourself
you will never be enough
for someone else

you must
want to spend
the rest of your life
with yourself
first

of course i want to be successful
but i don't crave success for me
i need to be successful to gain
enough milk and honey
to help those around
me succeed

my heartbeat quickens at
the thought of birthing poems
which is why i will never stop
opening myself up to conceive them
the lovemaking
to the words
is so erotic
i am either in love
or in lust with
the writing
or both

what terrifies me most is how we
foam at the mouth with envy
when others succeed
but sigh in relief
when they are failing

our struggle to
celebrate each other is
what's proven most difficult
in being human

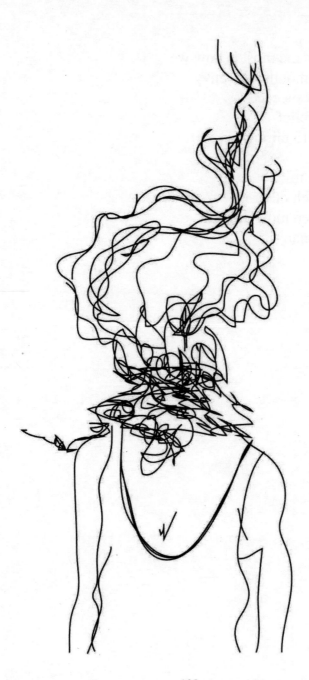

your art
is not about how many people
like your work
your art
is about
if your heart likes your work
if your soul likes your work
it's about how honest
you are with yourself
and you
must never
trade honesty
for relatability

- *to all you young poets*

give to those
 who have nothing
 to give to you

- *seva (selfless service)*

you split me open
in the most honest
way there is
to split a soul open
and forced me to write
at a time i was sure i
could not write again

- *thank you*

copyright

milk and honey
copyright © 2015 by Rupi Kaur.

Andrews McMeel Publishing

a division of Andrews McMeel Universal
1130 Walnut Street, Kansas City, Missouri 64106
www.andrewsmcmeel.com
www.rupikaur.com

ISBN: 978-1-4494-7866-7
Library of Congress Control Number: 2015946719
Ebook by Erika Kuster
ATTENTION: SCHOOLS AND BUSINESSES

Andrews McMeel books are available at quantity discounts with bulk purchase for educational, business, or sales promotional use. For information, please e-mail the Andrews McMeel Publishing Special Sales Department:
specialsales@amuniversal.com.

rupi kaur is a writer and artist based in toronto, canada. throughout her poetry and illustrations she engages with themes of love, loss, trauma, healing, and femininity. she shares her writing with the world as a means to create a safe space for progressive healing and forward movement. her creative direction and photography have broken international boundaries and have since made it into galleries, magazines, and spaces around the world. when she is not writing or creating other art, she is traveling to perform spoken word, as well as hosting writing workshops. you can find more of her work at: www.rupikaur.com

- about the writer